Testimo
Get Found Now!
Local Search Secrets Exposed

"A frightening book. If you own a small business serving a local community, after reading this, you will be shocked at how many free opportunities you may have left on the table. Covering all of the major search engines -- not just Google -- this very easy to read book spells out all the free things you can do today so that your business is found by prospects close by. Highly recommended."

-Liam Scanlan, Owner of Siteleads.net and author of Web Traffic Magnet (available on Amazon.com).

"Thanks to your book "Local Search Secrets Exposed" I got a high ranking on Google within 24 hours! Your book is a logical step-by-step guide to more exposure for any business. I had no idea how easily I could add my business information to so many free and significant on-line directories nor the amazing impact it would have. It's a tiny time investment with a huge payoff!"

-Tom Todd, Owner t2websites.com.

"Great overview on the merits of high placement in Google Local and how to get there. Thanks again for an excellent event. When I told my wife and daughter that you had used Brookside Dental as an example in your talk, they were very surprised but thought that it was very cool. I also have done the same thing that you suggested at Yahoo Local as well as Google.

I just posted our video from when we were featured on the TODAY SHOW at Google. Also, did my son-in-law, Brian Cave DDS, for his Edmonds Dental Practice in Google Local. He is number one for organic search in Edmonds and should move up very quickly for Local--we just did his yesterday. Thanks again. "

-Gil Pauley- Marketing Manager for Brookside Dental in Bellevue WA.

"Who knew that Local Search is such a complex and rewarding marketing tool? Richard Geasey and Shannon Evans, that's who! Every business owner should buy <u>Local Search Secrets Exposed</u> now. Make this easy to follow book a Top Ten business book and keep within reach at all times. You <u>will</u> be using it, especially if you want to be a small business success in your local area."

-Joanne Victoria, Author, Vision With a Capital V- Create the Business of Your Dreams. CEO, New Directions, Silverdale, WA

Get Found Now!

Local Search Secrets Exposed

Learn How to Achieve High Rankings in Google, Yahoo and Bing for Your Small Business

by

Richard Geasey
and
Shannon Evans

Copyright © 2009
Shannon Evans
Richard Geasey

All rights reserved. Any unauthorized use, sharing, reproduction, or distribution of these materials by any means, electronic, mechanical, or otherwise is strictly prohibited. No portion of these materials may be reproduced in any manner whatsoever, without the express written consent of the publisher.

All Trademarks are owned by their respective companies. We have no affiliation with any company mentioned in this book except our own or where noted.

www.practicallocalsearch.com

ISBN
1448614643
978-1448614646

Third Edition
September 2009

Cover Design:

Carrie Tatum
Bainbridge Island, WA

and

Richard Geasey
Shannon Evans

Dedication

As a twelve year old I was full of myself and quite the handful. I obviously was giving my parents a run for their money with my antics. I often slipped off to pitch pennies on the corner behind Big Star, ran up and down the river in a derelict johnboat with one good oar and the other missing the better part of the blade, and jumped off the trestle bridge into the Tombigbee River. I lived in cut-offs, dust covered ratty Keds, and a tank-style swim suit. I was a wild child and no matter how many dancing lessons, manners classes, fancy dresses, or days chained to a church pew my mother forced upon me, there was a restlessness that permeated my soul. Neighborhood moms must have dreaded my influence on their little darlings as I could make a grand and often dangerous adventure out of any lazy Mississippi summer afternoon.

After one particularly spectacular misadventure, I was sentenced to "house arrest" by my father. Part of my punishment was to read an Army manual he had on his book shelf (why he had it is beyond me as he was a 20 year + Air Force veteran). This particular manual was designed for NCO's and focused on leadership in the field. I lay on our porch swing and devoured that book. It was all about how to be competent, confident, and agile both in the field and in the heat of battle. I ate it up!

I still go back to that book for leadership principles and find the no-nonsense lesson it teaches applicable even in today's marketplace. My father probably has no clue the impact that one book had on me, but from this one simple book I learned what it takes to be a leader and how to be a leader of leaders. It taught me how to recognize leadership skills in others and how to interpret the intended and unintended consequences of certain leadership styles. I also learned another valuable lesson that summer day…my dad did know what was good for me! It just took me a few years of distance and perspective bring to recognize Daddy's wisdom.

Shannon Broocks Evans
Seattle, WA 2009

In 1988 I went to work for Western Digital, at that time a company providing storage controllers, Ethernet cards, Paradise video cards and other PC peripheral products (now they are one of about three hard drive suppliers left).
After a number of years in a variety of positions I ended up working for a gentleman named Jack Landau. Now Jack is a pretty smart fellow and I am sure I tried his patience on many more than one occasion (actually I know this for a fact). In our roles we focused on a variety of very large OEM customer meaning we generated a lot of written contracts, proposals and presentations.

I can recall vividly spending considerable time preparing some sort of document for Jack's review. A few hours later he would come in my office with my document virtually covered in red edits. He would drop it on my desk and say "this is pretty good". After more hours of fixing these edits I might get things done.
Despite my dejection seeing all those edits I did learn a few things from Jack. Hopefully they have been put to good use in this, my first book. So, I plan on sending one of the first copies to Jack. I'll be including a red pen so he won't have to look for one when he reads it!

Richard E Geasey
Seattle, WA 2009

"If you don't know where you are going, you might wind up someplace else."

Yogi Berra

Practical Local Search
Local Search Marketing and Consulting
Bellevue and Seattle WA

www.practicallocalsearch.com

Contents

Contents...1
Preface..3
Acknowledgements..4
Introduction..7
How Does Local Search Work...10
How Do They Know Where I Am..11
Keywords and Why They Are Important................................11
What is a Local Search Listing...14
Local Search- How to Setup Your Accounts..........................15
Google Local Business...16
How To Start Listing Your Business on Google.....................19
Keyword Identification 21
Google Local Business Center Listing Guidelines.................33
Notes, Warnings, and Cautions..35
Local Business Center Dashboard..36
Yahoo Local Search..42
Create Your Yahoo Local Business Listing............................44
Bing- Microsoft Local Search..47
Create Your Bing Local Search Listing..................................47
Other Information in Your Local Search Listing....................54
My Business Does Not Have a Fixed Location......................55
Reviews in Your Local Business Listing................................57
Local Search Goes Mobile..59
GPS and Local Search..61
Twitter and Local Search..72
Claim Your Listing or it Might be Hijacked............................79
Local Search Directories..85
CitySearch...87
Yelp...87
Insider Pages...90
InfoUSA...96
Local.com..100
Other Places to List Your Business.....................................105
Other Local Directories 107
Not in the US, What About Us..108
Optimizing Images for Local Search...................................108

1

Universal Search..109
Conclusion..117
Disclaimer...118
Need Some Help With Your Listing......................................119
About the Authors...120

Preface

In most cases today the first exposure potential clients and customers have with your business is via the Internet. You want to make a good first impression. To do that you have to control the content connected with your business, this is part of your overall web presence.

This book is focused primarily on the small business owner. Whether you own a brick and mortar establishment, are a service professional (contractor, financial, health care, services or others) or are in the hospitality business you will find the advice and suggestions in this book of great benefit to your business.

The great beauty of the information in this book is you do not need a web site of your own. Think how much fun it would be to rank ahead of competitors who have a web site! While these techniques will work without a web site of your own they are even more powerful and useful when you have one.
The Internet is the most powerful marketing tool of the modern age. It links buyers and sellers in a single environment. Unlike old methods of interacting with potential customers Internet local search has customers looking for *you*, not vice versa. Do your homework and control your web presence before someone else does it for you!
Take the time to read through this book a few times. Then spend maybe an hour or so to implement the suggestions. In some cases you will see results immediately. Good luck in building your business and its web presence.

With warm regards,

Shannon Evans
Richard Geasey

Seattle WA, May 2009

Acknowledgements

On a rainy day in late October I was teaching a workshop on how and why businesses should leave testimonials, and reviews on websites, local listings, blogs, etc. That was the first time my path crossed Rich's. He stayed for a about 10-15 minutes after class to ask some questions about my other workshops that I was conducting for members of a Seattle based networking group called Biznik.

Rich then signed up for my next workshop blogging versus micro-blogging. He also made an appointment to stay after class and discuss a "business idea." Over a great cup of coffee (this is Seattle after all) we talked about the idea of exploring a joint business possibility associated with web content for small to medium businesses.

After many meetings, additional cups of good and even great coffee, and many strategic planning sessions later, our business Small Business Marketing Tools was forged. This is one of several books in a series that came out of that first business meeting in the The Mosaic, a community church with a good little coffee shop.

I can't leave out Rick Eidens, my best friend and greatest cheerleader for tolerating the late nights I spend hacking away at words on my computer. I am so glad he loves cheese and crackers for dinner because many nights that was all I had time to help prepare. He is a saint with the best sense of humor when it comes to my moments of self-absorbed 'authorship'. Somehow he always knows when to show up with a cup of coffee or a shot of scotch as I muddle through edits, rewrites, and writer's block.

I also must thank my daughter Jennifer Evans for her professional editing skills and wonderful insights into the world of my audience. Her keen eye for what is right and what works (or doesn't) is much appreciated. I guess all that money spent on her tuition was well worth it! Perhaps this is a good place to thank all those teachers of mine who kept telling me I should "do something" with my stories, ideas, and observations. Miss Mary Cross, Miss Carnes, Mr. Locke, Miss Betty Lott...does this count?

~Shannon

When Shannon mentions meeting on a rainy day it makes it hard to pin the exact time down but I do remember it clearly. Since then we have started and have in process a number of projects we feel will benefit small business owners.

I'd like to acknowledge all of those business owners who have attended our events and helped make this book better. Many of them have actually taken our advice to heart and in fact have generated first page Google results. Good for all of you, and thank you!

~ Rich

Introduction

To say a small business owner has it tough today is a massive understatement. Competition from big box stores and the Internet continues unabated. Despite these competitive factors, most consumers still prefer to purchase their goods and services locally. And for many services you simply can't use the Internet. Can you get your garage door fixed on the Internet, get a massage, or unclog a toilet? Of course not!

Local businesses are the preferred purchase medium nearly 85% of the time. Even though the Internet is popular, most purchases are still done around the corner from the buyer. What is important now is how customers find your business, whether it is a store or a service. Increasingly, they are turning to what is called local search on Internet search engines.

In the past, when we wanted to find a business or service we pulled down the trusty Yellow Pages. The Yellow Pages are essentially a local search tool for potential customers to find the business or service they need. In the Yellow Pages, you flip through the directory to the listing meeting your needs.

You then have a list of business in that niche listed alphabetically (hence things like AAA Plumbing Supply). You'll also see a variety of listing formats. They range from a single line entry to quarter, half and full page ads. These ads represent search optimization (remember that phrase).

Substantially more than half of all searches are now done on the Internet. These searches are called "local searches" and the use of local searches is critical for your business success!

OK, why are they critical? Instead of being alphabetical in a book they are found via the keywords related to your business based on the proximity to the specific location in the potential customers' search. What do we mean by this? Let's take a look at a common search. A family just moved to Seattle,

Washington and needs a new dentist. They will use their favorite web browser and enter "Seattle dentist". This will bring up dentists in the Seattle, WA area. On the Google search page, there will be a display like the one shown here:

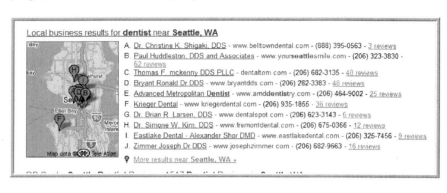

The information listed is typically pulled from various Internet listings (such as InfoUSA, YellowBook and Yellowpages), or is entered by the business owner. Notice the listing is not alphabetical; it is listed by what Google thinks are the best listings for "seattle dentist".

Now, here is where things get personal to your business! You as the business owner can completely control how this listing will look. And if you do a good job in creating a compelling listing then you could in fact have a number one listing in Google for your local business!

Now, think about this for a moment. No alphabetical Yellow Page listing, no inaccurate 411 listing, no pay-per-click advertising, no web site and *you* could have the number one listing! This is what this book is about, how to enhance the visibility of your business on the Internet when a potential customer searches for what your business offers.

The local search tools we'll discuss are relatively new and you may in fact find that you are the only one using them in your local market. If so, good for you! You will be able to beat your competitors and rank well without spending any money.

Wait, my business doesn't have a web site! Not every business needs a full-service website. Having a website is not the end all and be all of reaching your audience. Small businesses have to do more today than ever before to have a local presence on the net so their potential audience can find them.

Having a website is clearly an advantage; however, you can accomplish a lot without having a website if you follow a few easy steps to establish your local Internet presence.

How Does Local Search Work

We are going to dive into some background now. If you are not interested skip ahead to the "how to" sections. However, you might find it helpful to learn how the system works.

The folks running the Internet and the search engines are pretty smart. While they may lack some social skills and work at 2:00AM, they are doing some amazing things to help people find your business. There are four types of local searches:

Full Local Search- This is when a searcher types in a location and their search topic. Examples are "seattle dentist", "dallas pet shop", "boston steak house", and so on.

Partial Local Search- Many people simply type in their search term without an identifier. Use the previous examples but leave off the city name. The search engines know where you live (kind of Big Brother like) by the IP address of your computer. So if you live in Seattle and you type in dentist, it assumes you want "seattle dentists".

Destination Based Local Search- These are searches people use when they are going someplace. For instance if you are headed to Port Townsend (a popular getaway location for Seattle-ites) you may want to search for "Port Townsend bed and breakfast". This type of search, while not important for local searchers is critical for the weekend visitor or vacationer.

Pay-Per-Click Local Search- Pay-per-click advertising can also be used locally. Pay-per-click ads (Google AdWords primarily) can be specified to individual zip codes and other specific locations within a local area. If this is done, then these ads will only appear when a searcher is searching that specified area. Pay-per-click advertising is not really a focus of this book however, we will address briefly later on.

How Do They Know Where I Am

This is kind of scary to some; it's like the infamous Big Brother in 1984. The search engines know where you are by your IP address. Whenever a computer connects to the Internet it is assigned an IP address. It can be quite specific.

For most individuals and small businesses users, the detection of your location will be pretty accurate. For individuals behind a corporate firewall, it might not work as well. For the most part though when people do a search, the engines know you are in Washington State or Washington DC. This also applies to international locations as well.

Keywords and Why They Are Important

The Internet runs on keywords, plain and simple. Understanding this helps you create effective listings for your business. Remember, unlike the Yellow Pages where you have a section on dentists and they are listed alphabetically, the Internet works on what listings the search engine likes the best.

Let's go back to the "seattle dentist" listing again. Examine the "seattle dentist" listing below and you'll notice very few of the listings use the phrase "dentist", they use the phrase "dental". Do you search for a dental, or a dentist? In the world of Internet search, the listing with information best matching a search is usually listed first.

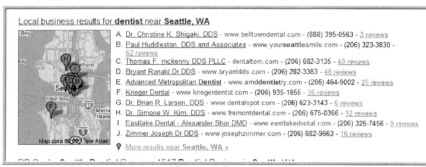

Dentist or Dental?

As you can see, most listings use the phrase "dental" or use the dentist's name or practice name or just "DDS". Now in all honesty, you would not search on any of these terms other than dentist! So, it is critical to understand how potential customers find you.

There are other important considerations as well. Misspellings can generate leads to your business as well. Different spellings of words can do the same. As an example one of the most common misspellings is jewelry (jewellry). Jewellry is the English version of our "jewelry", however many people spell it incorrectly.

Using this misspelling in your listing may help additional searchers find you. Another example is the phrase "steak house". This phrase can be used as one word or two. Search for "boston steak house" and "boston steakhouse" and you will see two different results. In fact "steakhouse" gets about 20% more searches than steak house.

Once you understand how your customers find you on the Internet, it is time to focus on the use of those keywords. Doing so will position your local search listings favorably against your competitors both big and small. You will also find this to be a useful exercise in regards to a web site, if you have one (that is a conversation for another day).

Another thing to consider is any specialties you might have. While you want to capture as many searches as possible, the more specific your service or niche the better your chance of capturing a high search ranking.

Again, let's use the poor "seattle dentist" example. If that dentist offers services to kids (pediatric), older patients (geriatric) or cosmetic services, they should create listings for those services. In this way, you will really out perform your competition. There are examples like this for all services and stores. Think what they might be and use them to your advantage!

What is a Local Search Listing

For virtually every business, the local search listing is derived from some database sitting on the Internet. When you conduct a local business search, the search engine goes looking for businesses that fit the keyword profile and displays them for the data it retrieves. In most cases, the data is accurate with a phone number and address. In other cases, there is additional information on a business (especially a restaurant) and that is made available as well.

The ideal situation is when you, the business owner "claim" or create your own listing. Sometimes, your business may not already be listed. This is common for one person professionals like consultants, therapists, trainers, coaches, etc.

The rest of this book leads you through creating local business listings on a variety of search engines and search directories. If you spend a reasonable amount of time in creating well crafted listing, your business will rank well and your potential customers will find you first in many instances in Google and other search engine rankings.

We should also mention a wonderful feature of these listings. For the most part they are free! What's not to love?

Local Search- How to Setup Your Accounts

Local search takes place on search engines like Google, Yahoo and MSN Live. Frankly, Google is hands down the easiest to setup and will be the most effective. However, Yahoo and MSN Live still provide another 25% of searches so we suggest you complete those entries as well. In this way, you are covered on over 90% of all Internet searches.

Another local search component is search directories. These include City Search, Yelp and many others. You'll also find valuable local search functions on sites like Judy's Book and Angie's List that track service organizations in regards to their performance (good and bad).

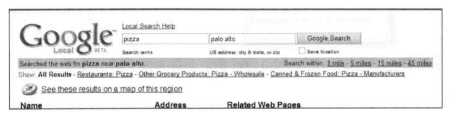

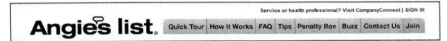

Google Local Business

Most of us are familiar with the normal Google search screen. Typically in the upper left section of the screen is the top listed result (everyone's goal). This is the natural search result and is the result of a lot of work by a web master to make sure that site ranks number one. Local search listing displaying in map format will supersede these results in some cases.

Now this is important! In many cases, your free local business listing will rank ahead of natural search listings and ahead of paid listings! And, you don't even need a web site! Google local business search is really a function of Google Maps, however these results do appear in the natural search page quite often.

A business that ranks high on Google Maps does much better on Google ranking overall. While Google gets dramatically more traffic than Google Maps, there is a symbiotic element at work here.

How does the algorithm for Google Maps work? The nice thing about Google Maps is that it is a fairly simple and straight forward data structure: location, location, location! Here is a simple interpretation:

"Local search needs specific data to work efficiently. Google must match the business to a location. When a user enters a business listing Google takes the data and associates the entry to a site on the map. If the business is listed in other listing servers and business data bases like Internet Yellow Pages or InfoUSA, it will often auto list the business by business name".

You don't have to have a web site to be found on Google Maps (or Yahoo! Local and MSN Live); however, if you do it needs to be optimized by keywords and location. Second tier local directories such as CitySearch, Yelp, and InsiderPages, citations, references and links from other web sites including your business name and location can improve your ranking for local search terms.

Customer reviews also help a business' rankings, but it is only a piece of the puzzle. Quantity and quality of the reviews count, but as to how they are ranked is anyone's guess.

Write a review

★★★★★ **Highly recommended!!** - A TripAdvisor Member - Jan 2, 2009
... I love this restaurant. The duck is magnificent. My brother in law whom normally doesn't enjoy duck loved it here. The Thai chicken sausage skewers were delicious as well. ...
Was this review helpful? Yes - No
More from Tripadvisor.com »

Write a review - Translate reviews

★☆☆☆☆ **Otis House Museum** - zabelle - Nov 27, 2007
... They have been returned to the time period of the Otis family. Most of the furniture in the house is of the period but not of the family. One exception is the dining room table which belonged to Mr. Otis' sister. The room colors ...
Was this review helpful? Yes - No
More from igougo.com »

★★★☆☆ **Frommer's Review** - - Jul 7, 2009
Legendary architect Charles Bulfinch designed this gorgeous 1796 mansion for his friends Harrison Gray Otis, an up-and-coming young lawyer who later became mayor of **Boston**, and his wife, Sally. The restoration was one of the first ...
Was this review helpful? Yes - No
More from frommers.com »

It is not clear what effect if any coupons have on ranking. It is assumed it does have an impact on ranking, but it is not clear at this point how much of an impact it has because it is a fairly new service.

How To Start Listing Your Business on Google

First, you must go to Google Mail (www.mail.google.com) to create a Gmail email address. This is a free service provided by Google. Once this is completed, go the main Google page (www.google.com).

In the top right hand corner there is a "sign in" icon. Click on it and this will take you to a log in page where you can create your personal Google Local Business account.

The Starting Point for Google

Select the "create one for free" highlighted icon in the middle of the page.

Create Your Account

Create a simple account using your first and last name or something easy to remember and a unique password. This will be your Google email account and access to all of the Google applications, including the Local Business Center.

Required information for Google account	
Your current email address:	
	e.g. myname@example.com. This will be used to sign-in to your account.
Choose a password:	Password strength:
	Minimum of 8 characters in length.
Re-enter password:	
	☑ Remember me on this computer.
	Creating a Google Account will enable Web History. Web History is a feature that will provide you with a more personalized experience on Google that includes more relevant search results and recommendations. Learn More
	☑ Enable Web History.
Location:	United States
Word Verification:	Type the characters you see in the picture below.
	Letters are not case-sensitive
Terms of Service:	Please check the Google Account information you've entered above (feel free to change anything you like), and review the Terms of Service below.

Create Google Account

Once you have established your account, you are ready to begin the basic keyword research for selecting the best words to position your listing.

Keyword Identification

As mentioned earlier, Internet search is keyword-based; therefore in order to figure out what keywords are best for your business, you will need to take a few minutes and do a little research and some word play.

The best tool (this is no surprise) is the **Google Keyword Research Tool**. This is found by searching in Google for the Google Keyword Tool.

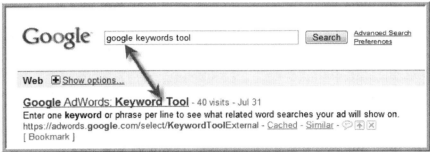

Google Keyword Tool

Enter your keyword to research in the box indicated and then type the characters in the window directly below the keyword entry box. This keyword should be what you believe is the number one keyword your customers use to find you.

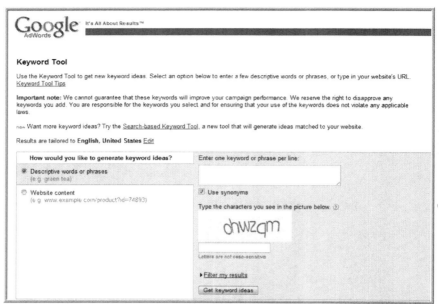

Using the Google Keyword Tool

As you become more adept with this tool, use more than one at a time and see how the results stack up against each other. You may be surprised to find that other words are more popular than the ones you believed to be so.

A list will pop up with the word you researched and its ranking as well as associated words and phrases with their position ranking. In the example below, the phrase "local search" was researched.

Keywords	Advertiser Competition	Local Search Volume: July	Global Monthly Search Volume	Match Type: Broad
Keywords related to term(s) entered - sorted by relevance				
local search		110,000	110,000	Add
local search guide		Not enough data	91	Add
local search tool		1,000	1,000	Add
google local search		5,400	8,100	Add
local business search		3,600	2,900	Add
local search news		1,300	1,000	Add
local search tools		Not enough data	91	Add
mobile local search		590	590	Add
local search directory		Not enough data	590	Add
411 local search		Not enough data	170	Add
local search advertising		1,600	880	Add
local search marketing		4,400	3,600	Add
local phone search		Not enough data	480	Add
beyond411 local search		Not enough data	22	Add
ebay local search		Not enough data	170	Add
www local search		Not enough data	1,300	Add

Keyword Tool Results

First, make a list of descriptive words for your business. An example is provided here for 'local search':

> local search, local search guide, google local search, local search advertising, local search marketing, etc.

Go through your list and select the highest ranked words that are closest in description to your business. Now that the list is made, you are ready to begin adding your local business listing on Google. Next go to "My Account" at the top right of any Google page.

Once there look for "Local Business Center " in the listing of tools:

If it is not listed there go back to Google search and type in "Local Business Center".

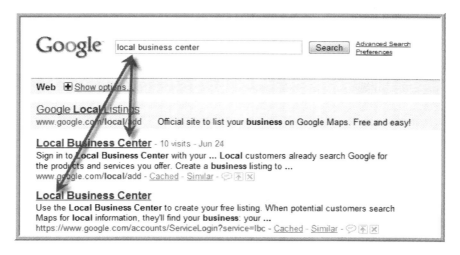

Once you add **Google Local Business** to your Google account page and select "Add listing". The following window will open:

24

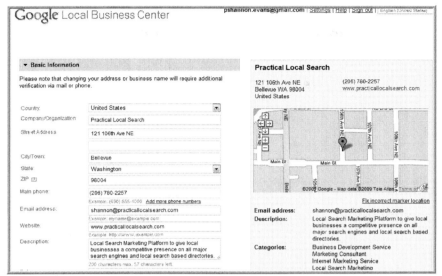
Basic Information Screen

The listing above has the company name included. Notice one of the key Google search terms is included in the listing name for the company/organization. It matches one of the key words in the description as well.

When you enter your company name, try to add a modifier using your number one keyword (if it is not already there). This is the entry your potential customers will see on the search listings, so make it shine! Remember, dentist, not dental (or whatever your situation is).

The description is another location for the highest keywords associated with the listing that you found on the keyword tool. Place them in descending ranking order. Keep things natural; don't just list every keyword you have.

You only have 200 characters here. I use Word to play around with my descriptions; it helps me easily count the words. I adjust the wording and keywords to get to as close to 200 characters as I can.

Once finished with that, you are ready to use some of the more prominent words you might associate with your business that is slightly different then what you used in your company name to categorize your business.

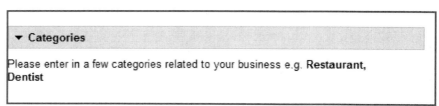

Create Your Own Categories

Categories are a powerful addition to your search options. Using your keywords create up to five categories highlighting your business. Categories is a way to get your secondary keywords in your listing. Google allows you to define your own categories, unlike Yahoo and Bing. Pay special attention here and you dramatically enhance your search success.

Practical Local Search's Categories

Practical Local Search used "Local Search Marketing" but also used "Business Development Services", "Marketing Consultant", "Internet Marketing Service", and "SEO" to categorize the business. You may have five per listing. You may select existing categories or create some of your own. Use as many as you can.

The next window asks for you to post your hours of operation:

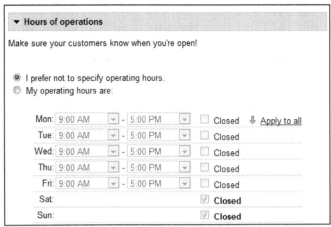
Hours of Operation

This is followed by how your clients can pay for your services and products.

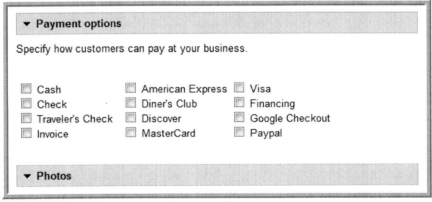
Payment Options

The next portion of your listing can be the key to real success when standing out from the pack. Adding video or photos to your site is incredibly important to making your listing literally leap to the front of the pack. It is a critical element to add if you can to promote your business. The photos must be related to your business directly and may even include a copy of your company's actual logo.

Videos can be loaded from the videos you have cross listed on YouTube. Incorporate as many photos and videos as you can. They actually work to optimize your ranking on the local search pages.

Bellevue, WA Art Gallery Listings

For goodness sake, if your business has graphical components to it then have photos and videos. Locally, in Bellevue, WA more than half of the art gallery listing do not have a picture. That's just crazy!

Your picture should be formatted to a three wide by two high ratio. If not, you'll get some "interesting" results. Any image manipulation program will allow you to crop or re-size your image.

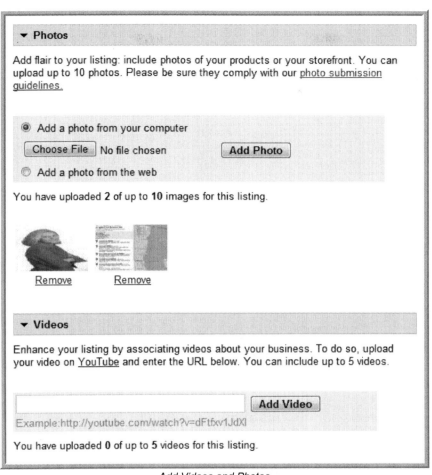

Add Videos and Photos

You can then add some additional information that might be helpful to your customers. Parking, special packages, associated brands, etc can be listed in the Additional Details section. You can create the additional listings and add the appropriate data.

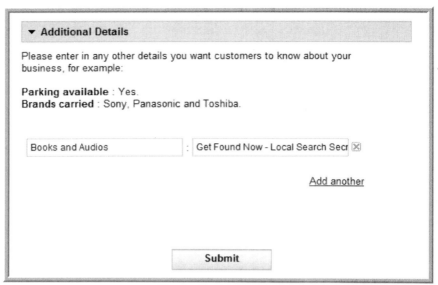

Create Custom Entries

After you have submitted your listing, you will get a notice instructing you to select either immediate contact confirmation with a PIN number or a scheduled confirmation call at a later date and time. Select what works best for you and you will receive a validation automated phone call. During this call, you will be prompted through a brief series of steps to enter your confirmation code.

Once you have confirmed your listing, it will be added or updated with Google Local Business search within 24 hours (sometimes it only takes minutes). You will also have the option to receive a snail mail notification.

You can have up to ten listings for your business, but the key is to change the company name just enough to keep the name original and add a keyword to the title. In the example above, the company name was listed as Practical Local Search. "Local Search" by itself has a high keyword ranking. Adding "Marketing" to the company name increases the relevance and ranking of the listing on booth Google Maps and Google Search.

Verify Your Location

You may also add a coupon to your listing. It is a nice touch for customers who find you this way. At the time of writing this book, we were not able to get a picture up loaded of a coupon. You may want to give coupons a try though.

Once you select "Add new coupon" a form will pop open where you can insert keyword packed details and a photo to create a customized coupon or coupons.

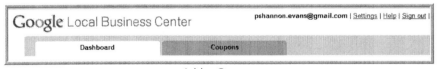

Add a Coupon

Here is another good place to include additional keywords that did not "naturally" fit in your description. It is also a great place to include other geographically targeted locations where you want to focus your business efforts to attract more customers and clients.

31

Provide enough details that clients and customers are enticed to use them and so that the search engines will find your coupon as well.

Coupon Form Field

What are some of the things you already give to your clients and customers as a value added business proposition? Do you discount first time customer purchases? Do you give a free assessment or free evaluation? What do you usually include as a part of your business and give to your customers? Is there a service you have considered discounting on a trial basis to attract more customers or clients?

The following coupon is a good example of a value added coupon. Red E Kleen Carpet has added Everett a commuter community north of Seattle to its coupon as a geographically targeted 'searchable' term for search engines. Additionally Red

E Kleen has added key search terms like "carpet", "upholstery", and "pressure washing" to enhance the listing.

```
┌─────────────────────┬──────────────────────┐
│  PRINTABLE COUPON   │ Good until Aug 29, 2009 │
└─────────────────────┴──────────────────────┘
Everett Red E Kleen Carpet
Cleaning
**15% off 1st time
customer**
Everett's Better Carpet Cleaner
```

Carpets, Upholstery, 24/7 Water restoration, Wood floors, Pressure washing. Get a bigger discount when using two or more of our services!

G41709

Google   77YG5CQFDCS7CNM1

Example Coupon

Google Local Business Center Listing Guidelines

Google Maps is a rich information source for both users and business owners. Every business in Google Maps listed through the Local Business Center must meet the terms listed below:

Guidelines: Google does have a few rules that are relatively strictly enforced. If not followed, all your business listings may be permanently removed from Google Maps. If in doubt whether or not a listing tactic is misleading, it is best to err on the side of caution.

The name on Google Maps must match the business name, this includes the address, phone number and website.

List information that is a direct a path to the business i.e.: official website pages and as exact of an address as you can.

- Only include listings for businesses that you legally represent.
- Don't create a listing for every town you service.
- Do not create multiple listings to cover all of your specialties.
- Use the description and custom attribute fields to include additional information about your listing.

In the case that your listings have been removed from Google Maps, then go in and edit them in your account to comply with their guidelines. Then you must fill out a **re-inclusion request** with Google.

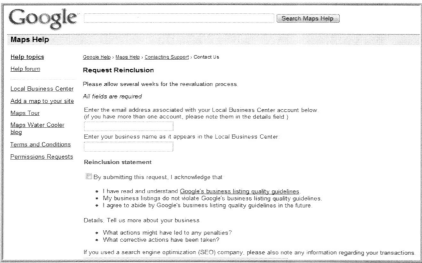

In Case You Need to Get Back In

Notes, Warnings, and Cautions

A few tactics you'll want to avoid with Google Maps:

Review Spam. Do not copy and paste reviews for your business from Google Maps on to other review sites like Yelp, Yahoo!, YellowPages.com, and City Search. This is considered 'manipulation' and will result in Google removing your listing from their site.

Duplication. You must be a bit creative and avoid excessive duplication of content. Avoid descriptions like: *Seattle SEO, Seattle Search Engine Optimization, Seattle Web Site Optimization, Seattle Optimized Web Site.*

Content Spam. If you change your company name from "John's Thai Food Connection" to "John's Seattle Thai Food Connection in Seattle", you will most likely get censored by Google.

Local Business Center Dashboard

One of the things to really love about Google is their focus on analytics and analysis. At the end the day most of us just wing it when it comes to deciding what works and what doesn't.

Once again Google is on top of things. In addition to their powerful and easy to use analytic tools for web sites they now have introduced a Dashboard based suite of tools for use with your local business listing.

This tool is free as well. If you apply the suggestions we make in this book, track your listing's performance using the dashboard and make adjustments as needed your local business and search presence will stay at the top.

Google Local Business Center Dashboard is a reporting tool for your individual local business listings. To access your dashboard go to Google.com and select "my account" from the top right corner of the page. Once you sign in you will be taken to your profile page:

Google Personal Accounts Page

Click on the Local Business Center icon. You will be taken to a new page with all your local business listing's dashboards:

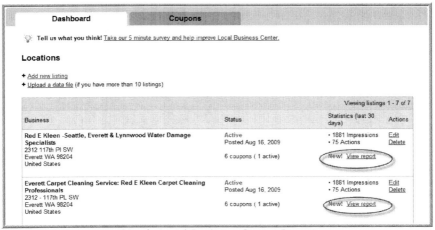
Google Local Business Center Report

Click on "view report" and you will be taken to a new page full of useful tracking information about your business listing. It reveals real statistics related to your listing.

Google Local Business Listings Statistics

This report shows how many times users found your business listing as a local search result. It also shows how many of those then clicked over to your business listing.

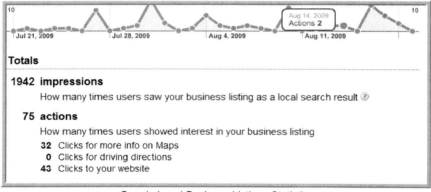

Google Local Business Listings Statistics

Below the local business listing statistics are the individual search queries (keyword phrases) used to find your listing.

The report shows:

- Specific number of times your business listing popped up on a search result in Google.com or Google Maps over a specific period of time.

- Specific query keywords used in finding your business listing.
- Number of users who actually took action with the listing (clicked to website or requested directions).
- Zip codes of users asking for direction

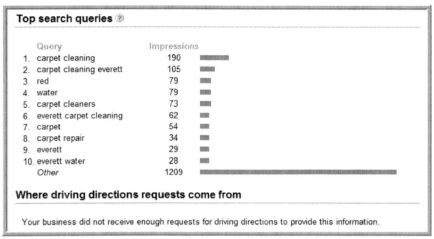

Google Local Listing Dashboard Results

The best part about this information is that you see how many users clicked for more information on the map about your business listing, how many clicked for driving directions, and best of all how many then clicked over to your business website. It also shows where the driving directions came from:

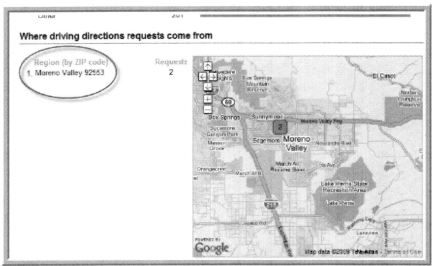
Google Local Search Driving Directions

The information included in the dashboard is not the same as the results you get with Google Analytics on your actual website. This is only a resource tool related to your Google local business listing. What it does do is provide you with information that can be useful in helping you attract more customers. This reporting mechanism shows exactly how Google users are interacting with each of your local listings. You can use this data to help you optimize your local listing by analyzing your keywords and the resulting traffic.

The savvy business owner will use this information to identify customer search trends related to their listing. It also helps them to refine their listing in such a way that it enhances the traffic to their listing. Now there is a real-time method to measure impressions, actions, and location before and after new marketing campaigns. This tool will help you decide on the most effective keywords and categories for your local listing.

The data is updated daily so you should be able to quickly identify what is working for you in your local search listing. Currently the data is not exportable but hopefully it will be in the near future. Other possible upgrades in the dashboard might show you which keyword in the local search lead to which action and the geographic location where the search originated.

Yahoo Local Search

Yahoo Local is really simple to set up as it has only two text fields; one for what you're looking for and the other is where. In the default home page, Yahoo displays a lot of local information to help you get started, user reviews of local businesses, and an invitation for you to add reviews to Yahoo Local. There are RSS feeds and links to various categories of local businesses as well.

Yahoo devotes most of its space to business listings and reviews, and displays small map on the left side. Paid ads are much more prominent on Yahoo Local than on Google. These ads come from Yahoo Search Marketing's Local Advertising Program.

Their search parameters pick up far more unrelated businesses then on Google. For example, if you are looking for Real Estate broker you will also get paid listings for Real Estate Attorneys, Real Estate Appraisers, and Real Estate Wealth Building Books and Software.

Yahoo Local is user-driven. User rating reviews are included with each business listing where available, along with comments and feedback by Yahoo users.

Yahoo Local free business listing includes:

- Business address, phone number, your domain name
- Listing in up to 5 categories
- Feature your products, services, brands, etc

For an additional fee you can add more features to your listing like logo, photos, branding tag line, coupons, etc.

It is interesting to note that things that are free in the Google Local Listing cost extra on Yahoo.

Create Your Yahoo Local Business Listing

To begin, check to make sure your business is listed in Yahoo Local and that the information is accurate. To do this, go first to the Local Listings Center and look for the free "Local Basic Listings" option. You do not need a Yahoo account to do this. The submission process is easy to follow, and takes place completely on-line. When you're done, Yahoo says your submission will be reviewed for inclusion within 3-5 business days.

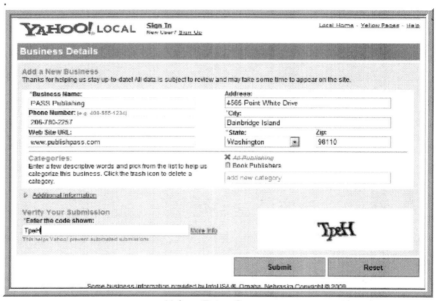

Yahoo Entry Screen

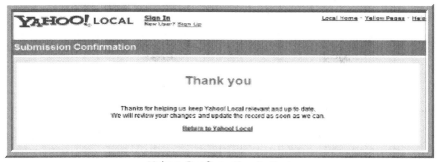

Yahoo Confirmation is Fast

You can also sign up for either a "Local Enhanced Listing" or for a "Local Featured Listing." For a flat fee, these services will add keyword enhancements to your Local Basic Listing.

Yahoo Search Marketing also offers "Local Sponsored Search," a pay-per-click advertising option that targets your ads in the geographic area(s) of your choosing. This does not require you to have a web site because the program includes a "locater page" that displays all your physical business location and contact information.

It isn't the review star ratings that are important...it is the fact that you get a review posted that adds to your ranking. Referrals from satisfied customers have always been the best method for generating new customers. They are a powerful method to establish credibility and to instill a sense of security in new customers.

Bing- Microsoft Local Search

Bing is the new Microsoft search "engine" (they call it a decision engine). There is of course a local search component. It is a relatively simple text field application with several links to add extras like directions, business categories, detailed business listings, and user-created map content.

Bing's local search results page implements a two-column approach that is similar to both Google and Yahoo local search. On Bing's site, the first column shows business listings (and paid ads), the other uses Microsoft's Virtual Earth service to exhibit the exact locations of those listings on a map.

Create Your Bing Local Search Listing

Add your business listing at Bing's Local Listing Center. To begin, first check to see if your business is already listed. If it is listed, a few tweaks to optimize the listing is all you will need to do. If it is not listed, the listing process is simple. With Bing, you can add additional web page URLs, email addresses, business hours, accepted payment methods, tagline, and up to 10 photos of your business, as well as a few other niceties.

You will need a Hotmail account to get started. To keep life simple, use the same login format you used when you created your Gmail account and just tweak it so it works with Hotmail.

Go to <u>Bing</u> and select the icon in the top left window that highlights Hotmail.

You Need a Hotmail Account First

A new window will open and you will select the sign up icon.

Go Ahead and Sign Up

This will take you to a standard form where you will create a unique account and password (hopefully one that you will remember). Perhaps you will want to use a combination of your name and your company name. Make sure it is something easy to remember or else write it down and leave it where you will remember where you have it so you can update the listing from time to time.

Create a Windows ID

Once you have an account, you can then go to the **Bing Local Business Center** to get started creating your local search business listing.

Bing Search Page Results

Select the Bing local listing domain name to begin.

Live Local Listing Center

Click the "add new listing" icon and you will be taken to the page where you first check to see if you business listing is already cached.

Local Listing Entry

If it does exist, you will move to a new field where you can edit your listing (or create a new one).

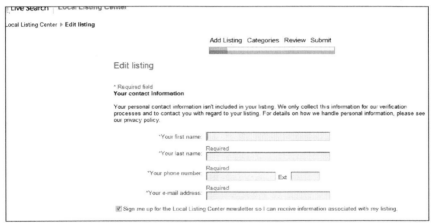
Ensure Your Information Is Correct

Then you can begin categorizing your business. Remember to categorize it from the perspective of the potential client or customer who is seeking your type of services.

How will your customers begin their search on a categorical level? Bing does not allow you to create your own categories.

Unfortunately, it's been our experience the categories are simply not adequate for many purposes.

Select Categories

Once you have made all your selections and submitted your input, you will be taken to a review page.

Verify the Physical Location

52

Carefully review the listing for accuracy to verify the red pin is in the correct location as well. Submit the location page you will be taken to a standard terms of agreement page.

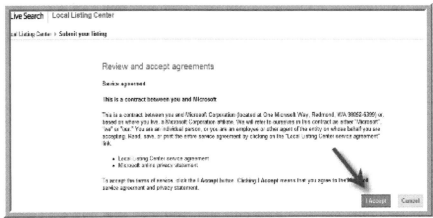

Accept the Agreement

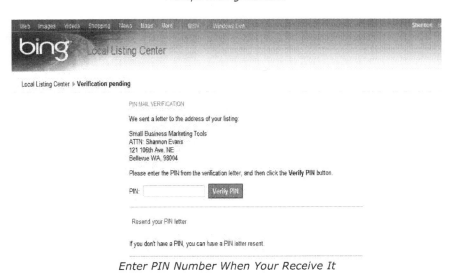

Enter PIN Number When Your Receive It

After you've submitted a new business listing, Bing Local will send you a confirmation code by mail. It takes about 2-3 weeks for it to arrive.

Follow the directions on the card to enter the code back into the Local Listings Center to confirm your business listing.

Other Information in Your Local Search Listing

You will find in your local search listing other information you did not enter. There may be photos and reviews from other web sites. This is normal and it will help your search results.

Photos will appear in your listing from anywhere there is a photo relating to your business. This is primarily accomplished when you have a website that other sites refer to (called back linking).

Local Search Listing Photos from Third Party Site

In the example above for the top listed Chinese restaurant in Seattle in Google Maps, you'll see that all photos are from other web sites. In this case (when this was done), it seems the business itself has not completed a local search listing.

As you can also see in the previous image, there are 79 reviews and 71 instances of user content. User content links to this site or address that does not originate from another web site. In this particular instance, these links come from citations in Google Maps.

For users of Google Maps, you might know you can link a picture to a specific address on Google Maps. What tends to happen with these User Content links is individuals have created collections of Google Maps links to share.

There are dozens of people with Google Maps lists showing the best jazz bars in Dallas, the best Chinese restaurants in Seattle, etc. The nice thing is you are getting free links. These instances are typically focused on the hospitality and entertainment industry. It's not often you see a collection of favorite Chicago tax lawyers!

My Business Does Not Have a Fixed Location

Some businesses don't have a fixed location (except where a bill is sent to). A recent email from a mobile dent repairer highlighted this issue. In some cases you may use your home address to deal with this issue. We don't suggest this option for personal security reasons. If you only have a personal address consider purchasing a PO box from a third party (not a USPS box). If you already have a PO box call it a suite, not a box. Add the street address as well and you will have a solid location for your local business listing. The following few paragraphs provide some additional thoughts regarding the location of your business and the impact on your local search success. You can simply use a PO Box if you don't want potential customers trying to walk in.

Generally the location being searched is the primary determinant of success in a local search. And why not, if you are looking for a business in Seattle WA you are not likely interested in driving to Bellevue (or from Dallas to Ft. Worth, and so on) to find what you are looking for. For most businesses (stores, professionals, contractors and others) who have been around for years, there is not much you can do to optimize your location, You are where you are! New businesses, however, may want to consider their location of record (license, mail delivery and website contact page) as part of their selection in where to lease or buy space. In the larger metropolitan areas it's likely being inside the city limits will bring you more success with on-line traffic.

While distance from the city center seems to be on the decreasing as a factor in local search success, the strength of the location in the search results poses a major problem for mobile service-based businesses who visit their clients, rather than having customers come to them. After all you don't visit the plumber to get your toilet unclogged! Adding to the issue is these mobile service providers are frequently in lower cost areas, or areas with more room for their equipment that are well outside the city center. Yet the businesses still do the bulk of their business in the city area.

The most popular way around this problem is for the savvy business is to purchase a PO Box or UPS Store address in the cities in where they desire to rank. There is some evidence this is declining in popularity, however it remains a technique that when coupled with optimization of the rest of your listing will result in success. As with most areas of local search just don't get carried away and open multiple PO boxes throughout the city.

Note: Using a PO box with a local phone number (using Skype for instance) a business can open a virtual location in another city and achieve search success. This is handy for service providers who want to open up new areas without actually establishing a direct physical presence.

Reviews in Your Local Business Listing

Reviews (or citations) are wonderful to have in your listing. They instill confidence in your potential customer, allow existing customers to express their experience and best of all provide extra "juice" to your listing when search engines evaluate your listing. Like other elements of your listing, reviews are compiled from all over the web. People can also leave reviews directly in your local business listing if they have an account in Google (or Yahoo or MSN). You will also find when a local business has not "claimed" their listing, the overview section will likely be populated with reviews if they are available.

The important thing to remember about reviews is that they tend to be a tie breaker in ranking a certain listing. All things being equal, a listing with more reviews will tend to rank higher. And in a twist of irony, bad reviews count the same as good reviews. I suppose that supports the theory that there is no such thing as bad PR!

We recommend that you should solicit customer reviews. They help potential customers make a decision to do business with you and that is an opportunity that should not be missed.

Third Party Site Reviews

You can make it easy for customers to leave reviews Add links to local consumer review sites on your website. Offer an incentive to leave a review. Here are a few sites to provide links to:

- Citysearch.com
- Google Maps
- InsiderPages.com
- Judy's Book
- Mojopages.com
- Yelp.com

Local Search Goes Mobile

I recently purchased one of the new **Google G1 Android based phones**. Wow, what a revelation! Even though I have been in high technology for over twenty five years I was still surprised at the power of this hand held device.

It has all of the features of any other phone, a keyboard and of course Internet capability. I found a neat feature and it's called Voice Search. By speaking your search into the phone it will perform searches similar to what we have discussed in this book so far. Now, I'll say it does not work perfectly, however in about seven of ten tries it gets it right and up pops your search. When it doesn't I just try again.

The screen display does not include the map listing you have become familiar with however it does include the business name, the star rating and the number of reviews. There is the phone number so you can instantly dial the company and directions which will feed the GPS on the phone. This is a very convenient and powerful feature. The phone knows your location so essentially all searches are local in nature.

The advent of mobile local search is another reason to optimize your local search listings. Handsets are only getting more powerful and this feature will become more robust over time.

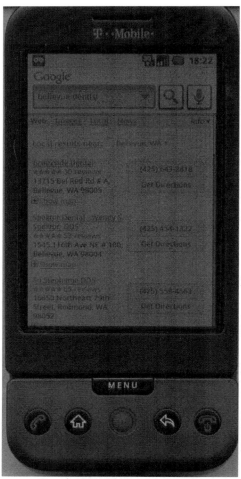
Google G1 with Search Results

Tremendous numbers of people will find soon enough the power of these new handsets and to a certain extent they will rival a laptop for many functions such as searching the web and email. Don't miss out on this chance to position yourself at the top of local search results and take advantage of the mobile search crowd.

After I discovered the voice feature I learned about another very cool feature for using any mobile phone with text capability. By creating a text message with a local search phrase (such as the Bellevue dentist we used previously) and sending it to 466453 (google) you will receive a text message back within a few seconds with between one and four results. They will be similar to what you would see in a normal Google search on your PC as far as who is number one.

GPS and Local Search

Mobile search capabilities are only going to get more powerful so be sure to have your local search profile and optimization process completed and maintain it regularly to keep your ranking intact. One growing opportunity is your (and potential customer's) GPS unit.

More and more new cars come equipped with GPS receivers and new car owners have come to rely on them as their main navigation tool. Dashboard GPS databases are now filled with points of interest (POI) that are now easy for businesses to update or even add business listings. Portable GPS units now are in the $200 range for a nice one and under $100 for a decent one.

Have you or your customers tried to find your business with GPS? Just because you can't find your business on a GPS device does not always mean it is not to be found there. Your business may just be a point of interest that wasn't included by major mapping companies in all their recent programs or updates. You may be listed at the wrong address, or you may be in the database but under the wrong category! So…how do you get your business "on the map?"

First, you want to make sure you are included in the mapping databases. The three major databases are NAVTEQ, TeleAtlas, and InfoUSA. There are some niche POI data providers that with a little searching you should be use to your business's advantage. Updating your listing can be a bother but we have included a few pointers to help you with the process.

NAVTEQ maps is a major provider of maps for mobile devices including Garmin and Nokia. They are the largest in-vehicle navigation system data provider for web and location based mapping in North America. They are the "Google Maps" of GPS so this is the place you want to have your business listed first as a POI. Go to www.navteq.com to access their site. Select Map Reporter to update or enter your business listing.

NAVTEQ Home Page

A new window will open. In this window you can either update a location on an existing listing or you can create a new listing for a business.

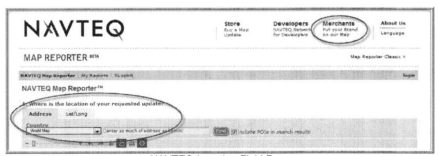
NAVTEQ Location Field Page

The Merchants – Put Your Brand on the Map feature is no longer active. Instead, follow the directions in the form field on the lower half of the screen. First select the Point of Interest icon in the "type of feedback" section of the form.

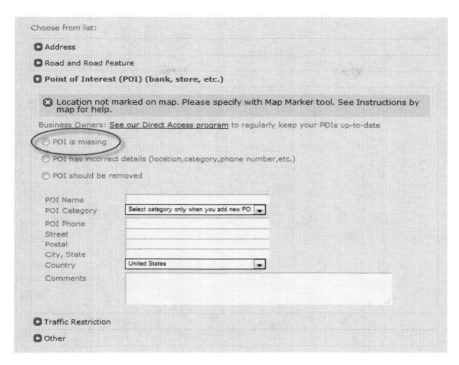

NAVTEQ Address Form Field

Enter your address and if it does not recognize it, select a listed address that is closest. You will be given an opportunity later to move the "pin" to your exact business location later.

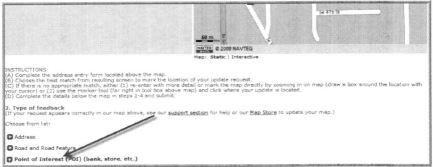

NAVTEQ Point of Interest Form

A new window will drop down with a form field to fill out. Include keyword rich material in your description.

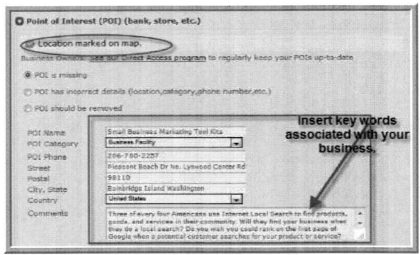

NAVTEQ POI Form Field for Specifics

Once you have finished entering all critical information all that is left is to click to submit. It takes several days for the information to populate their system. It also relies in some cases on the users updating their systems via downloads; however, in many cases the systems automatically refresh information when the user turns on the device for their next "session" of use.

TeleAtlas is another GPS mobile locater service. Go to: www.teleatlas.com/index.htm.

Report Map Changes

Begin by selecting the language you wish to enter your information into the database:

If your customer base is from a diverse population you might consider providing listings in multiple languages. After you select the language for your listing you will be taken to an entry page. Select the "start" button to begin:

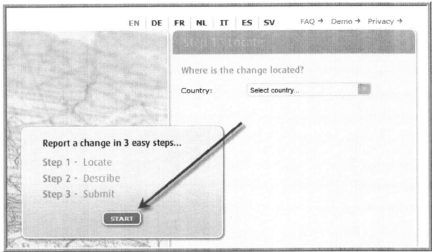

Teleatlas Start Field

You will then be directed to indicate where the point of interest (your business) is located. We used a business in Seattle, WA so the United States is our country of location.

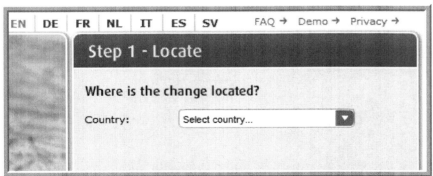

Teleatlas Location Field

We then entered the exact street location:

Teleatlas Street Address Form Field

You can also give exact latitude and longitude if you happen to know them for your address; however, they are not required. You are then required to move a push pin from the left side of the map to the location of the point of interest on the map. This is a "click and drag" feature.

Teleatlas Click and Drag Map

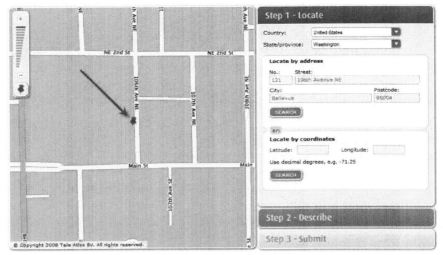

Teleatlas Pin Location Field

Your pin is now in place where your business address is physically located, now you must give the atlas the specifics of your point of interest.

To the right of your map is a series of six button boxes. To add your business to the database with a description you must select "Point of Interest."

Teleatlas Point of Interest Selection Field

68

A new window will open with two choices:

- Add a point of interest
- Change a point of interest

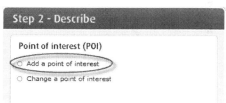

Teleatlas Add Point of Interest Field

Select "add a point of interest" if this is a new listing. You will then be taken to a form field that asks for the name of the POI and a brief description. Fill that description with keywords related to your business that tells who and what you are.

Teleatlas Point of Interest Description Field

After entering all the necessary information click on the Step 3 Submit bar at the bottom of the page. This will take you to a page to review your listing as it will appear on the various GPS and mobile devices. You will be required to supply an email address for site verification at this point prior to final submission.

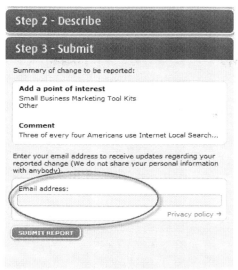
Teleatlas Email Address form

Teleatlas then updates their database and sends the information to GPS locater databases, Google Maps, other mobile device database companies, on-line shopping guide databases, etc. Every time a company or device owner downloads new maps, they are getting downloads of the latest updates from databases like Teleatlas. This makes it incredibly easy and inexpensive to maintain up to date listings for your company as it grows and changes location, etc.

It is important to keep in mind that just because you can't find your business on a GPS device doesn't necessarily mean it isn't on the map. It just might not be on that particular GPS device. The GPS manufacturers don't include every POI due to storage space limitations. If you want to do your part to make be sure you've got a shot at inclusion list your business with the major mapping companies. If you don't, it is unlikely that they will move to include you!

Twitter and Local Search

Most of you have heard of **Twitter** by now. It's in the news far and wide and you may be wondering whether it's for you or not. This section is not meant to be the definitive guide or how to section on Twitter, there is plenty on that elsewhere. We will however mention a few very specific purposes for using Twitter in relation to local search results.

Attaining a high ranking in the search engines is the purpose of all we have discussed up to this point. The use of Twitter is simply another element to this. It has been reported in some instances a Twitter account can rank highly in search results. While this is not all that common yet it is clearly something to consider.

Even if you do not plan to "tweet" yet, we advise at least capturing Twitter account names relevant to your business. There is no cost to obtain a Twitter account (or more than one) and it makes sense to own it before this technique becomes more popular.

Twitter names should be a combination of your top business keyword and a geographical tag. Twitter names such as @bellevuedentist, @austinrealestate and @syracusepetstore if used actively at some point may in fact provide an additional highly ranked placement in the search engines. There is a 15 character limit for your Twitter user name, so get creative. There is also a 160 character limit on your description. Be sure to remember to make judicious use of your most effective keywords (including your location ones).

As an extra bonus, as Twitter becomes more popular and you elect to tweet you may gain additional business from using Twitter above and beyond just the boost in local search results. In the following example you will see how a Papa Murphy's Pizza store in Knoxville TN is using Twitter to promote their store (with a plug for the NCAA Basketball tournament as well).

This screen shot is from early April 2009 and they really don't have that many followers. However over time this could easily change dramatically and this local store might rank higher than other larger chains.

Papa Murphy's Knoxville TN Twitter account

Twitter now has location based API (an open programming interface for developers) letting users filter their searches by location. If you are a brick and mortar business or an online business with a local presence consider selecting a Twitter account name with a local flavor.

For example, if you are a dentist in Bellevue, WA why not snag the Twitter name "Bellevue Dentist". Your profile will have your real name and your URL as well as a brief description that you provide so there is nothing potentially stopping you from using the power of local search in your Twitter moniker.

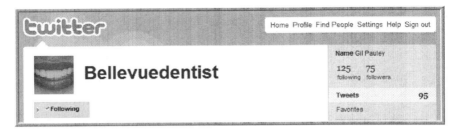

Once you have established your Twitter persona you will want to cultivate your local presence by connecting with others in your community. You can use applications like Summize to search for other local Twitter users by searching for them by city name, user location, etc. You can then begin to follow and respond to local search queries with a direct message.

For those who elect to send and receive Tweets via their cell phones, local search not only shows which service type businesses are Tweeting about their specials. The great thing about SMS Tweeting is that not only does the message show up on the screen but the phone number does too! Soon they will be Tweeting restaurants reviews too.

Who is tweeting near you? Twitter local is a great tool that lets you search use geo-targets. You can use RSS feed to monitor Tweeters locally. Try a search on Twitter that is geo-targeted: "Restaurant Seattle". Restaurant is the most frequently used local search term. Test it for yourself and see!

How can a business use local search to their advantage on Twitter? First, create and publish a Twitter business page so people can communicate with you. Link to your business website in your profile. Perhaps use your logo or a photo of your store front as your avatar (profile picture) so people will come to recognize you by sight. Then get people talking about you.

Let's say your restaurant is the Salty Dawg Diner in Seattle. Your Twitter name on your profile could be "saltydawgdiner." Your patrons can promote you on Twitter with messages like, "I just ate fish and chips @saltydawgdiner with @localsearchsea!"

Perhaps you can offer a special discount to patrons who will Tweet from the table for the server on their iPhones. Ivar's (a popular seafood joint) in Seattle did this recently to celebrate their founder's birthday:

> Happy 104th Ivar! Mon 3/23 get special. Buy entree, get 2nd for $1.04. 3/23 only. Say "Happy b-day Ivar" 2 get it.
> http://tinyurl.com/d92rsb
> *1:10 PM Mar 20th from web*

Really creative businesses can combine traditional local search with their current discussions by intertwining it in the conversation. If it is a listing, event, or even a classified type listing with a little imagination you can work it in easily. For instance, "New camera's with polar lenses on sale tomorrow @SeattleCamera."

Try something with a little more creative edge to garner local reviews, ratings, anything that can be geographically targeted. "Saw new play @MillCityPierTheatre with @shannonevans and was not impressed." Or, "The ice @skateoutsideSeattle is perfect tonight."

To take advantage of local Twitterers' regional expertise you will need to court them. Follow them and send them special direct messages (DM) thanking them for their follow backs. Make your interaction with them through @replies, DM, and your Tweets conversational and personal to the local customer. Talk to your customers and tell them useful information that helps them keep you in mind as their local choice. Ivar's in Seattle does this to perfection in their tweets:

> @Andersonimes Either Acres of Clams or Salmon House are great. +Both have awesome Happy Hour from 3:00ish 2 close, 7 days/week. KEEPCLAM
> 10:26 PM Apr 18th from web in reply to Andersonimes

Make your messages specific to your locale. Offer them incentives, ask them for feedback, give them simple surveys that allow them to voice their opinions and to provide their uniquely local incite.

Cultivating your local presence on Twitter helps you not only to build brand reputation but to also build Google search engine results. Twitter related Google listings result when you Tweet with locally targeted messages.

It creates a better user experience for your community when they can relate to your messages. When you embed geo-targets (location names) in some of your messages it increases traffic generated by local search and when you have more traffic you increase your user base and ultimately your market share.

Help your business use Twitter effectively to attract local business. Treat your customers with respect and ask for their advice and opinions about your goods and services. Acknowledge your customers as individuals and use them to check your company's social pulse. If you do that you will reach individual communities with your unique message that is personalized for that audience. Invite customers to respond, give feedback, and offer criticism so you can uncover and address any issues that might lay hidden beneath the surface.

Share useful information and ask for community involvement and your company's local presence will expand exponentially.

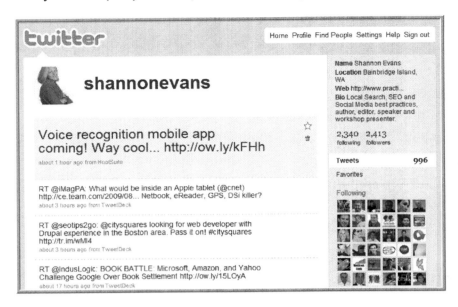

Claim Your Listing or it Might be Hijacked

When someone says hijacking, do you think of a terrorist barging onto a plane and flying to Cuba? That's not what we're talking about here! We're talking about a nasty trick where someone steals your business identity on Google Local Business.

How does this happen? It's actually pretty simple. Until you "own" your Google Local Business listing anyone can come in and make changes to it as if they were you.

When businesses are presented in Google, the data is typically pulled in from other online resources such as InfoUSA or YellowPages. While this is fairly bare bones information, it should in most cases be an accurate reflection of your business name, location and phone number. You can find your information by searching for your business name or address in Google Maps.

So, how can my listing be hijacked? Anyone can go into a Google Local Business listing and claim it as their own. The hijacker creates a Google email address and then a Local Business Account. They find the listing they want and change the phone number and the URL of the business (or add one if there isn't one). The hijacker also slightly changes the address so Google thinks it's actually a new listing.

Google provides a phone verification process and bingo, your listing is hijacked. Subsequent to this, your business name could also be changed and you are now gone from view by Google searchers in your locale!

While your business may still be found by other means, a good number of searches may be hijacked to the "new" bushiness phone number and URL. This causes lost sales to you and potential confusion to searchers. There have been some organized attempts at this in San Diego to florists, locksmiths and Pay Day Loan operations. In the floral instance, the URL was directed to a Canadian on-line florist, who ended up stealing a lot of business.

Here is a good example where some Seattle metro businesses had their listings hijacked:

Recently I needed my carpets cleaned in my home. I went on line to find a local carpet cleaning company to call for estimates. I noticed that the first three listings were toll-free numbers and not local listings.

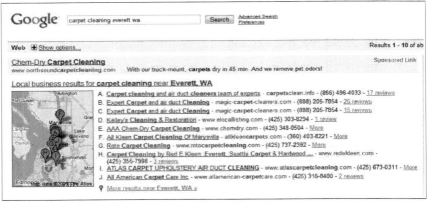

Carpet Cleaner Everett

So I called the first number just to see where they were located and as I suspected they were not truly "local" at all.

I dialed the first number and a man answers, "What do you want?" I thought to myself this guy is not really professional. Strike one for customer service. I asked, "Have I called the Carpet Cleaning Experts?"

He responds even less professionally, "Lady, what do you want?" Strike two for customer service.

I took a deep cleansing breath and asked, "Where are you guys located?"

"All over the place!" he snapped impatiently.

"Could you be more specific?" I asked innocently. He hung up. Strike three!

Suspecting that this was actually a referral site that sells leads to local carpet cleaning companies I 'clicked' on their link to find out more about the company and their actual location. Here is their website contact info:

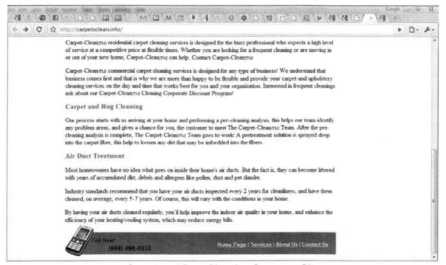

Carpet and Duct Cleaning Company Site

No address, no email information...this was not of much help. I still know nothing more about the company.

I then looked more closely at the actual local business listing that was on Google. Notice the name at the top of the listing and the associated website. Then look at the associated reviews:

Carpet Cleaning Local Listing Street Address

Something does not work here! So...I dig deeper in the Google local listing to find out more about their services from the actual listing. I was really surprised to find that the 'Overview' tab revealed reviews for a Restaurant/Pub called 'The Flying Pig!' The reviews were interesting - some good, some bad but nothing that had anything to do with carpet cleaning or duct work cleaning.

Mismatched Listing

So now I go back to the top of the listing and look at the street address for the carpet cleaner:

Street Address of Hijacked Listing

Then I go and conduct a Google search to see if the Flying Pig Restaurant has a local listing. Do they even exist? Are they really in Everett?

Flying Pig's Actual Local Listing

Notice the website? These guys are good! They have hijacked The Flying Pig's site, built a new one that uses the restaurant's reviews for search 'juice' and the restaurant's address to anchor the reviews and give them the appearance of a center of Everett local listing. These guys are good!

These guys have stolen not only the Flying Pig's listing but that of several other area restaurants that have not claimed their local listing either:

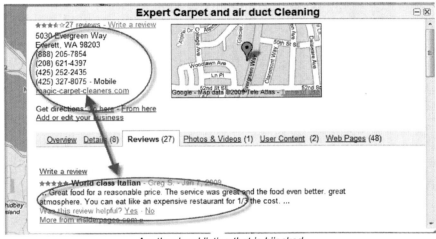

Another local listing that is hijacked

Maybe these guys can feed you while they clean your carpet?

Is this happening a lot right now? No, however once the word gets out that this is possible, it will occur more frequently. The real worry on a local basis is your competitor changing your information (URL and phone number) to theirs. They could even change the location to theirs and you would disappear!

How can you prevent this from happening? The most important thing to do is to claim your business listing on Google right now.

Local Search Directories

Local search directories play an important part in this process. In many instances, the search engines get their data from these directories. Even after you edit or create your own listings, you will still see data from these directory listings appear in your local search listings.

Most of these directories are national in scope, but have local directories for each major city. If you search in any major city for restaurants, clubs and bars, you will find many of the top listings come from these directories.

Like local search, you'll want to ensure that you control what is presented and how well. Notice in the Google search "seattle chinese restaurants" that all of the top listings are from a local search directory.

Some of the directories have free options and some have paid options. Evaluate how well they will serve you and your business and determine which might be best for you. Clearly you can't pay for all of them; however, some searching on similar establishments might give you an idea of which ones are the most appropriate for your business.

Google

seattle chinese restaurants   [Search]   Advanced Search / Preferences

Web

Seattle Chinese Restaurants: 10Best Restaurant Reviews
Get **Seattle Chinese restaurants** in **Seattle** WA. Read the 10Best **Seattle Chinese restaurant** reviews and view users **Chinese restaurant** ratings.
www.10best.com/Seattle,WA/Restaurants/Chinese/ - 50k -
Cached - Similar pages

Best of Citysearch Seattle 2009 - Best Seattle Chinese Food
Best of Citysearch **Seattle**. Visit Citysearch to find the best **Chinese** Food in **Seattle**, plus the best **Seattle restaurants**, bars, night clubs, hotels, spas, ...
seattle.citysearch.com/bestof/winners/chinese_food - 64k -
Cached - Similar pages

Seattle Chinese Restaurants on Citysearch
Looking for **Chinese Restaurants** in **Seattle**, WA? Find reviews, maps and directions for **Seattle Chinese Restaurants** on Citysearch.
seattle.citysearch.com/yellowpages/results/Seattle_WA/page1.html?flavor_id=2&cw1=23 - 115k - Cached - Similar pages

Chinese Restaurants in Seattle, WA on Yahoo! Local
Chinese Restaurants in **Seattle**, WA on Yahoo! Local Get Ratings & Reviews on **Chinese Restaurants** with Photos, Maps, Driving Directions and more.
local.yahoo.com/WA/Seattle/Food+Dining/Restaurants/Chinese+Restaurants - 103k - Cached - Similar pages

Seattle Chinese Restaurants - Seattle.com
Seattle Chinese Restaurants. Add your organization or business ... **Seattle**, **Chinese Restaurants**. Bell Thai Thai Restaurant. 2211 4th Ave, **Seattle**, ...
www.seattle.com/chinese-restaurants/business-directory 31k -
Cached - Similar pages

Seattle Chinese Food in Seattle WA Yellow Pages by SuperPages
Directory of **Seattle Chinese** Food in WA yellow pages. Find **Chinese** Food in **Seattle** maps with reviews, websites, phone numbers, addresses, and business ...
www.superpages.com/yellowpages/C-Chinese+Food/S-WA/T-Seattle/ - 181k -
Cached - Similar pages

Seattle Chinese Restaurants | Yelp
208 businesses reviewed for **Chinese Restaurants** in **Seattle** on Yelp. Read about places like: Sichuanese Cuisine **Restaurant**, Mandarin Chef, Szechuan Noodle ...
www.yelp.com/c/seattle/chinese - 43k - Cached - Similar pages

Google Search "seattle chinese restaurants"

CitySearch

CitySearch is a major provider of local information for sites including MSN, Ask.com, Expedia.com, Ticketmaster.com, and others. It is a fee based listing and expensive to maintain. It has a basic and a premium pay fee.

Yelp

Do a search for your business name and zip code to find out if you're already listed in Yelp. On the bottom of the search result page, you'll see a red button titled ADD BUSINESS which leads to a simple form where you can add your business.

Begin with creating a Yelp Business Owners account at www.biz.yelp.com.

Initial Account Info

Create your listing using your unique business name and tie it to a keyword from your previous search when creating your Google business listing. This will take you to a standard form

(The example below added "Book" to the publishing company name):

Enter Your Company Name

A listing of related businesses in the selected city will pop up after selecting the search icon:

Add Your Business

If your business is not listed, click on "Having trouble finding your listing?" A new window will pop open where you will now enter all your pertinent business information.

Enter Basic Business Information

An auto response will pop open that requires you to verify the listing via an email sent from Yelp.

That's it. You are now listed on Yelp. Now, you should send your clients and customers over to leave a review of your services.

Insider Pages

Insider Pages is owned by CitySearch. It works by combining local listings with user-generated reviews. Access their site to see if your business is already in the Insider Pages' database.
If your business is not listed on Insider Pages, go to www.insiderpages.com and click on "join now".

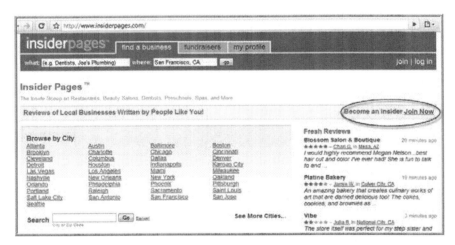

Create your account profile using standard information found on any application.

Enter Your Basic Information

Once you click on the "join" icon, a "Thank You" page will open. In the "what" window type in your business name and in the "where" window insert the city where your business is located.

A listing window will pop open with your business name, followed by a list of related business names. See if your business is listed; if it is not, go to the bottom of the page and select the "add a business" icon.

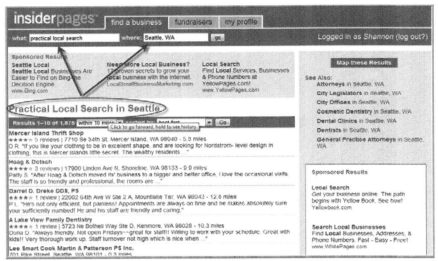

Example Information

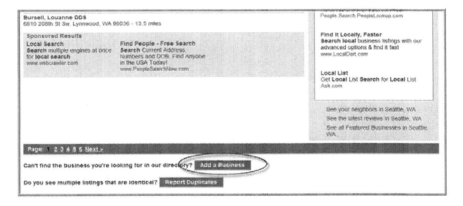

A new window will open that allows you to enter information about your business, as well as to select two business categories from their selection list that describes your business. While the list is somewhat limited, you can be fairly creative in manipulating it to your advantage.

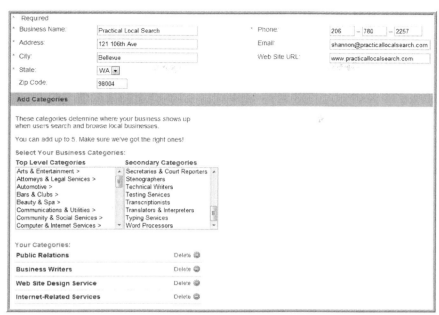

Add a New Business

Once you enter the information, the next window will ask you to "claim your business".

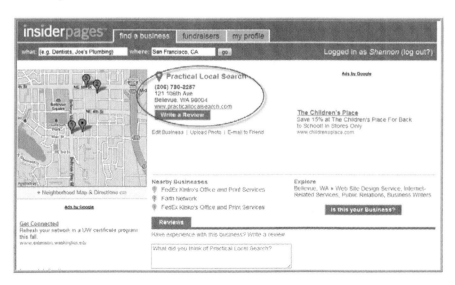

A confirmation window will pop open. This gives you an opportunity to make any necessary changes to your listing or to send emails to customers to request reviews of your business.

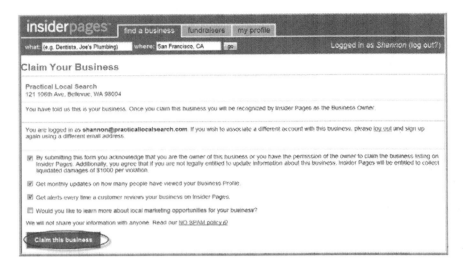

Carefully check the listing information provided and then select the options appropriate for your business needs and then click on the "claim this business" icon at the bottom of the page.

Once "claimed" you will be taken to a confirmation page where if you feel you need to tweak your listing you can go back in and edit your listing.

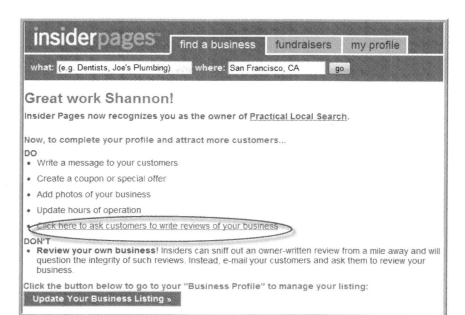

InfoUSA

InfoUSA is an information collection site that maintains databases on businesses in the U.S. and Canada. It collects information from white and Yellow Pages, business records, etc.

There is a good possibility that your business is already in their databases; however, if it is not already listed or if an existing listing requires editing, go to www.infousa.com and scroll to the bottom of the home page click on "Update My Listing."

A page will pop open where you can add or change your listing.

The listing window will open and a form field will appear to enter your business information.

Add Your Company Information

A second window will pop open, listing subcategories for your business listing. You only get one choice, so choose well!

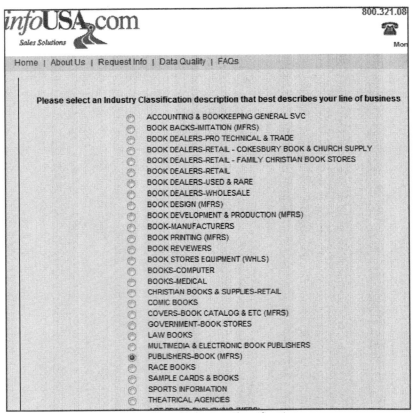
Enter Your Industry Classification

After you select your more refined descriptor, you will be directed to a page where you can add additional pertinent information about you and your business.

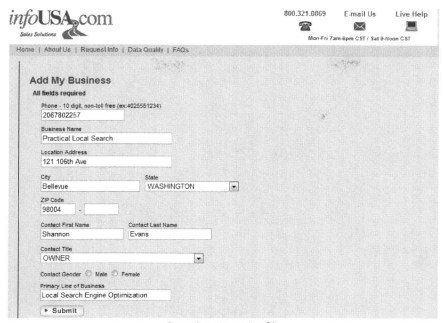

Complete Your Profile

That is all there is to their listing process. The listing will take quite a bit of time to be posted, up to 60 days.

99

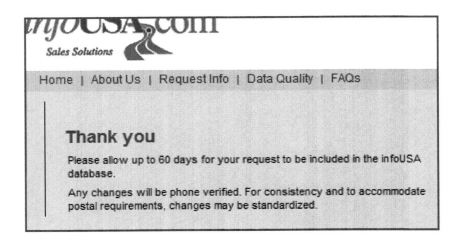

Local.com

Local.com is one of the fastest growing local search engines with almost 10 million visitors per month. The site posts user reviews from sites such as Insider Pages and Judy's Book. There is a free basic listing and a premium option that costs about $40 a month. To begin the listing process, log onto www.local.com and the home page will open. Click on the "Get your business listed on Local.com" to begin the process.

Add Your Business Information

100

A basic form field will open asking for your business name and location.

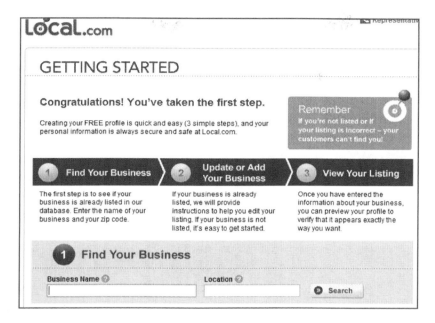

If your listing is not found, you will be directed to the "Find Your Business" page. Select the "Add Free Listing" button to add your business.

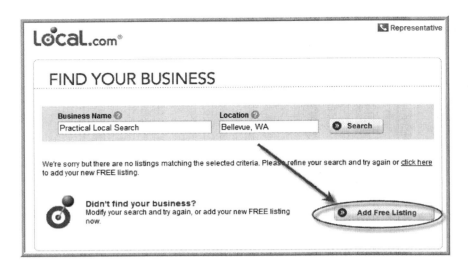

Add your pertinent business information in each of the form fields on the Free Listing entry page.

Add Your Listing

You will then be directed to a business category page. Enter key words related to your business and the "Possible Categories" field will begin to populate with categories. You will be allowed two for posting purposes.

Select Your Category

After you submit the listing, you will be sent a confirmation note directing you to confirm your account from your email account.

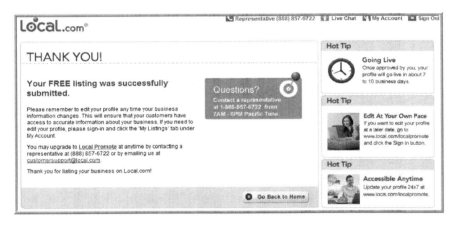

Other Places to List Your Business

There are literally thousands of local directory sites. There are many specific geographic ones (say for a single city) as well as for specific business niches. Bottom line, you need to know how your customers typically look and find you on the Internet.
If a particular directory constantly shows up with your competitors, then you may want to consider adding your listing to it.

Two other directories to be aware of are **Judy's Book** and **Angie's List**. Both are focused on service industries like contractors. Unfortunately, they began as a place to leave information about bad service providers. Over time, listings have become more balanced however; many people use them to leave bad reviews.

Judy's Book

Remember the old line about how a happy customer tells one person and a mad customer tells ten? Well, this is magnified today! Judy's Book collates reviews from other sites and allows users to leave their own as well. Angie's List is a paid service.

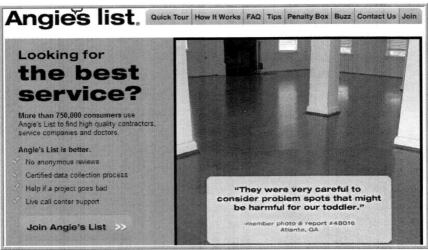

Angie's List

Other Local Directories

There are other local search engines out there that are city or region specific. A quick search using your community name should reveal other sources like www.seattlebusinesslist.com. There are literally tens of thousands of search engines and directories on the Internet today and many have local search components.

Not in the US, What About Us

As you certainly noticed all of the information in this book focuses on the US, and more specifically the Seattle area. With all of the rain and snow during the winter of 2008-2009 we had plenty of time to write this. However, if you are not in the US you may be wondering if these techniques will work for you. The answer is absolutely yes.

For the most part these techniques and processes will work worldwide and in any language. In fact, in smaller countries and locales you may find the techniques being especially effective as there is less awareness from your potential competitors. So take the time regardless of where you are in the world and take a couple of hours and lock in your local search position today.

Optimizing Images for Local Search

We all want to beat our competitors using particular keywords hoping to dominate our own niche markets in Google's Universal search listings. Most companies attempt to take advantage of Google to improve their exposure in the market place and to attract new clients and customers using SEO tactics; however, they often fall short because they do not take advantage of all the Google Search options a business can use to coordinate with their local search optimization efforts.

Google is now using a blended result list when a visitor conducts a search. You will first find the paid results (Adword driven indicated by the arrows on the right in the graphic below) then in the left column of the page will be any local listings that can be mapped (not always present), followed by a mix of Products, Images, Blogs, News, Video, and Business listings (geo-targeted). This helps visitors on Google find what they want without having to leave the organic results page.

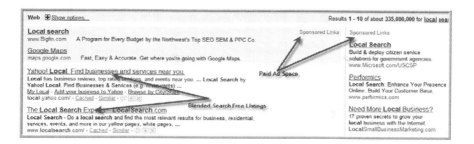

Universal Search

Universal Search is Google's attempt to figure out what the user is trying to find in the search results. Is the person conducting the search looking for a business near them? Are they looking for a particular type of product? Are they looking for a specific product using a model number? How searches are conducted reveal much to the developers at Google and their competitors search sites.

Why is this important for local search? Because your website, your product catalog, and your local business listing all "talk" to Google if they are optimized correctly. What does that mean exactly for a business owner trying to have a solid web presence for their goods or services? It means opportunity!

Businesses, if they are smart about their listings and their content now have multiple ways to position their goods, products, and services on the first page of Google.

Some businesses, using geo-targeted (location names) keyword rich file names may now see their images, videos and products listed on the first page of organic results certain search terms.

Google has a central page from which to access all the universal search tools. Go to the Submit Your Content page and you can get started:

www.google.com/submityourcontent/index.html

Google Universal search has multiple avenues for related search efforts:

- Google Image Search
- Google Video
- Google Product Search
- Google News
- Google Blogs
- Google Maps

Google Image Search is easy to manipulate for optimization purposes. Use a descriptive file name.

Instead of *image1.jpg* try *local search-book-cover-1.jpg*. Use ALT & TITLE tags, with about a five to ten word description, the more descriptive the tag the better.

Add descriptions under your image on your web page and in your local listing images. Incorporate a geo-targeted word in each of those descriptions:

File Names- Accurate names are important. If your photo is of a navy blue double breasted blazer name your image navy-blue-double-breasted-blazer.jpg. Targeted relevant terms help you defeat the competition in search terms.

Image Alt Attribute- Provide a good, solid description of your image using the image alt attribute. Use product color, size, brand, material, etc. Accurate thorough product descriptions create relevancy for search terms. The Alt tag is easily added in virtually every web page editor using the image properties option.

Captions- Caption your image with related descriptions. The text that surrounds the image helps Google to understand the image's subject.

Anchor Text- The text you use when linking to the image describes and classifies the image. Use descriptive anchor text instead of "click here", "larger image" or "more photos" when describing a link.

Google Image Labeler- Improve your chances of having your images appear in Google Image Search by permitting others to classify your images with Google's Image Labeler. Google Image Labeler allows users to provide words and phrases they think best describe your images in an on-line "game". As users are shown images from your website, they type in a few words to describe the photo. These descriptions are later used to classify your image.

In order to upload video to your local business center listing it should be under 100 MBs. First you must load your video directly from your browser to YouTube. Create a title and description for your video that is keyword rich and contains a geo-target. The title, file name, and description of your video are critical for your being found in local search results.

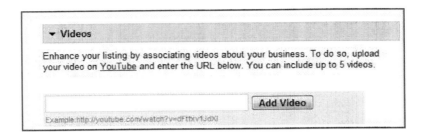

Google Product Search helps you with your organic and local search rank. In order to have your products listed in Google Product Search you must first establish a feed of your products. Each product title should contain keywords that help sell your product.

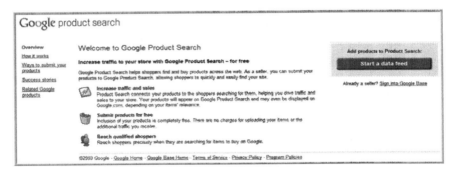

You must update your feed about every 30 days by changing titles. Frequent feed updates help you get and maintain better ranking on Google Universal Search. It is also helpful to constantly add new products.

Google News is a great place to get your company press releases posted. Nothing helps your business rise in the public eye and in the search engines like good press. There are several ways to get in Google News but basically, to get listed in Google News is to have original content, proper attribution of all sources, keyword rich title and keyword rich copy.

From the publishers help page select "submit your content":

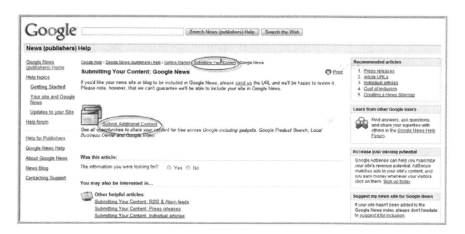

Select "Google News" and a new page opens with more specific directions for uploading your news or blog feed.

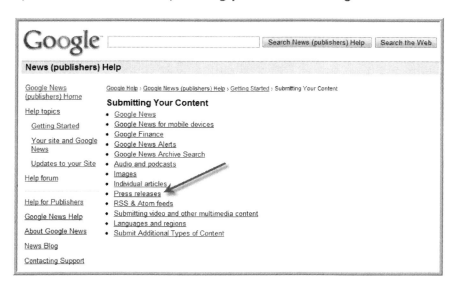

Go to Google Blog Search to add your blog to Google's search directory: http://blogsearch.google.com/ping?hl=en

Google's Blog Search is a great place to manually submit your blog. You really do not have to submit your site for it to be indexed by Google; however, it sure makes it faster to get listed! It is as simple as adding your blog's domain name and hitting submit!

Google will find your blog through its frequent crawls. One of the ways to help Google find your blog more easily and more quickly is to gather quality incoming links. Back links is one of the factors that determine a blog's rank.

When searchers type in a business name or brand name is the end user trying to see a picture of the product or a review of it? Are they trying to make a purchase or just do background research of the product or the brand name? Google Universal Search returns search results that attempt to meet all those requirements.

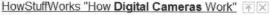

Pretend you are shopping for a new digital camera. If you enter "digital camera" in the search query you will see Google Products listed at the top left of the screen: Web, Shopping, Images:

Google pulled in organic search results, Google Product Search, *and* Google Images with the search term "Digital Camera."

> Unbiased **Digital Camera** Reviews and News: **Digital Camera** Resource Page
> The **Digital Camera** Resource Page has been providing unbiased **digital camera** reviews, news, discussion forums, buyers guides, and frequently asked questions ...
> www.dcresource.com/ - 43k - Cached - Similar pages -
>
> Shopping results for **digital camera**
> Canon EOS **Digital** Rebel XTi **Digital camera** - SLR - 10.1 Megapixel ...   from $430 - 25 stores
> Canon PowerShot SD750 **Digital** ELPH **Digital camera** - compact - 7.1 ...   from $150 - 60 stores
> Canon PowerShot SD1100 IS **Digital** ELPH **Digital camera** - compact ...   from $140 - 63 stores
>
> Canon **Digital Cameras**
> Shoot with ease and style with the Canon PowerShot **cameras** including **Digital** ELPH series. PowerShot **digital cameras** incorporate the creative performance of ...
> www.usa.canon.com/consumer/controller?act=ProductCatIndexAct&fcategoryid=113 - 98k -
> Cached - Similar pages -
>
> KODAK EASYSHARE **Digital Cameras**

You can move ahead of your competitors if you know how to target traffic with Universal Search resulting in better ranking and more exposure. Google also lists blogs, books, and other related listings:

You can possibly receive a first page listing on Google if in your listing you optimize your images, submit your keyword rich product descriptions on Google Product and optimize your local business listing with video and good targeted descriptions.

Google has provided many new opportunities for you to reach searchers in the ways they want to be reached. Search engine optimization has been taken to another level; it's no longer about who has the most number of pages, the best density; or who has the most inbound links. It is about who is utilizing all their available opportunities.

Almost every aspect of your website is being analyzed and classified; use it to your advantage. Now is the time to take advantage of these opportunities and improve your visibility in every area of universal search; allowing you to grow your traffic and exposure in new and exciting ways.

Conclusion

As you can see from all the local business listing agencies popping up on the Internet, having a Web presence that you can control to some extent, can be critical to your success. Keeping the conversation going about you and your products and services is critical now, more than ever. Continue feeding and nurturing your web presence through local listings and watch your presence and your business grow.

Validation of your business information by you, third party reviews and articles gives you control over your business information and prevents competitors from hijacking your results. This gives your business credibility on the web when your basic business data is consistent from source to source. It is crucial to your rankings and to eliminate the possibility of wrong information being connected to your business.

Differentiate your business from the billion other businesses on the Web and make it easy to find you and your business using local search. You as a business can nurture and maintain your presence on the web even if you don't have a website. Create your local presence and watch your business grow!

Disclaimer

The techniques discussed in this book are designed to achieve more exposure for your business in search engines such as Google, Yahoo and MSN Live. However, as best intentioned as these techniques are and as many times as individuals and businesses have had success with them, there is absolutely no guarantee of any success at all.

The ranking of any search engine listing is a mystery to every one except for the engineers who created the algorithms. What works one day might not work the next, a long held position may disappear tomorrow, and your listing may appear at the top almost immediately but not show up a week later. No one knows for sure what works perfectly every time.

What we do know is by applying the techniques outlined in this book you will create the best opportunity for success. In most cases, you will see improvement in your search rankings. Like most things in life simply getting in the game helps enormously.

Good luck!

Need Some Help With Your Listing

If you would like come help in creating a highly optimized local search listing for your business, large or small contact us. We provide consulting and preparation services will help your business Get Found Now.

Prices vary on depending on what coverage you desire. Some options include:

- Keyword research
- Google
- Yahoo
- Bing
- Search directories like Yelp, Yellow Pages etc.
- 411 directories
- GPS directories
- Dashboard analytics review

We offer assistance in setting up your YouTube channel and creating images and videos for upload to your account.

If you would prefer to let our fingers do the typing then contact us at info@practicallocalsearch.com.

About the Authors

Practical Local Search
Resources for Small Business Marketing

Practical Local Search is a Seattle based company focused on developing and publishing ebooks, books, DVDs and seminars focused on small business marketing on the Internet. We strive to provide quality resources for small business owners looking to effectively compete on the web. With considerable writing, publishing, marketing and business experience small business owners will find materials and expertise to compete against local and on-line competitors.

Richard Geasey- Co Founder, Practical Local Search

Richard has a more than 20 years in the high technology industry with additional time in international trade development and small business consulting. Richard's career actually began in the military as a Captain in the Field Artillery where he learned being cold, tired and living in substandard housing was no fun. He transitioned to high technology in 1981 selling mini computers to construction companies. Moving to the high tech giant Hughes Aircraft Company he realized a big defense company was even less enjoyable than the Army.

Finally he found a home at Western Digital in Irvine CA just as the PC computer industry really started to take off. Starting as a product manager for WD's line of Ethernet cards he ended up handling major OEMs as a marketing manager. When the Ethernet business was sold to SMC Networks he continued his work with the likes of IBM, Dell, HP and other large companies and he had the good fortune to manage International marketing for a number of years. Sadly the fun began to wind down as the hardware business turned to lower and lower margin sales. Time with Seagate Technology and tape backup drives surely highlighted that! Five years with Lantronix focusing on device marketing lead to some interesting markets like industrial automation, medical devices and other fun segments and wrapped up his hardware career. He does have a lasting legacy as the inventor of the world's only Internet BBQ.

The last few years saw time with the Australian Trade Commission as a Business Development Manager based in Seattle. In this role he worked with dozens of small Australian businesses as they created export opportunities to the US and specifically Seattle. Since then he has focused on working with small local businesses and writing books on SEO, importing, marketing on classified ad networks and local search. He also skis, bikes, hikes, plays golf and backpacks in the beautiful Northwest.

Find me on LinkedIn at: www.linkedin.com/in/richgeasey
Email: richard@practicallocalsearch.com

Shannon Evans- Co Founder, Practical Local Search

Shannon Evans is contributing author and editor of *Your Ultimate Sales Force* and multiple business. Her books teach entrepreneurs that they must publish or perish in the Internet age where businesses must deliver a consistent and unified message. This is especially critical in this challenging environment of email, Internet, and mobile phones. Leveraging the market today requires new methods for attracting new clients. Shannon is recognized in the Puget Sound as an expert in how to make your business have a web presence rather than just a web page. Her conversational marketing techniques and practices outlined by Small Business Marketing Toolkits will see your small business presence on the web increase.

Shannon's workshops and discussion groups are much admired by local and national professional networking groups. Whether coaching entrepreneurs on the ins and outs of writing a white paper or in how to create a website that sells, her classes are all well attended and often standing room only. Her frank, down to earth approach to Internet optimization demystifies the terms SEO and SEM for the layperson and leads the participants to a hands on session that makes them go from being one of a million to one in a million on the web.

Shannon has a wide and varied background in both the practical and the pragmatic aspects of the business world. As Co founder of Small Business Marketing Toolkits she loves nothing better than teaching local businesses how to think globally but to be searched locally. When she is not writing or teaching she can be found coaching boys' lacrosse, biking, fishing or clamming somewhere in the Seattle metro area.

Find me on LinkedIn at: www.linkedin.com/in/pshannonevans
Email: shannon@practicallocalsearch.com

Other Books by Shannon Evans:

- Your Ultimate Sales Force: 159 Strategies to Generate Referrals and be Worthy of Them
- Twitter: Building Your Business Presence Using Social Media
- Email Signatures that Sell
- Online Marketing Campaigns
- How to Create a Killer Media Kit
- Thought Leader or Blowhard? How to Write a Book that Enhances Your Professional Credibility

Other Books by Richard Geasey and Shannon Evans:

- E-books- Writing Copy that Sells Electronically (publication date – Summer 2009)
- Building Your Business Presence on the Web – Using Social Media to Make a Name for Yourself (publication date – Fall 2009)

Finis

Made in the USA